中华人民共和国文化部
2015年文化发展统计公报

STATISTICAL COMMUNIQUÉ OF THE MINISTRY OF CULTURE OF THE PEOPLE'S REPUBLIC OF CHINA ON CULTURAL DEVELOPMENT IN 2015

中华人民共和国文化部　编

中国统计出版社
China Statistics Press

图书在版编目（CIP）数据

中华人民共和国文化部 2015 年文化发展统计公报：汉英对照 / 中华人民共和国文化部编 . -- 北京：中国统计出版社，2016.4
ISBN 978-7-5037-7778-3

Ⅰ . ①中… Ⅱ . ①中… Ⅲ . ①文化发展－统计分析－研究报告－中国－ 2015 －汉、英 Ⅳ . ① G12

中国版本图书馆 CIP 数据核字 (2016) 第 090342 号

中华人民共和国文化部 2015 年文化发展统计公报

作　　者 / 中华人民共和国文化部
责任编辑 / 郭　栋　李　冲
装帧设计 / 黄　晨
出版发行 / 中国统计出版社
通信地址 / 北京市西城区月坛南街 57 号
邮政编码 / 100826
办公地址 / 北京市丰台区西三环南路甲 6 号
网　　址 / http://www.zgtjcbs.com
电　　话 /（010）63376877　63376907（发行部）
印　　刷 / 北京画中画印刷有限公司
经　　销 / 新华书店
开　　本 / 880×1230 毫米　1/16
字　　数 / 50 千字
印　　张 / 2.5
版　　别 / 2016 年 4 月第 1 版
版　　次 / 2016 年 4 月北京第 1 次印刷
定　　价 / 28.00 元

目录

CONTENTS

中华人民共和国文化部 2015 年文化发展统计公报[1]

2015 年，全国文化系统全面贯彻党的十八大和十八届三中、四中、五中全会精神，深入学习贯彻习近平总书记系列重要讲话精神，紧紧围绕“四个全面”战略布局，坚持社会主义先进文化前进方向，坚持以人民为中心的工作导向，开拓创新，积极作为，文化改革发展取得新成效，“十二五”时期各项任务圆满收官，为建设社会主义文化强国、全面建成小康社会、实现中华民族伟大复兴的中国梦奠定了坚实文化基础。

一、机构和人员

2015 年末，纳入统计范围的全国各类文化（文物）单位[2]29.91 万个，比上年末增加 1.18 万个；从业人员[3]229.44 万人，增加 25.42 万人。其中，各级文化文物部门所属单位 65714 个，增加 152 个；从业人员 64.53 万人，增加 7124 人。

图 1　2006 年 –2015 年全国文化单位机构数及从业人员数

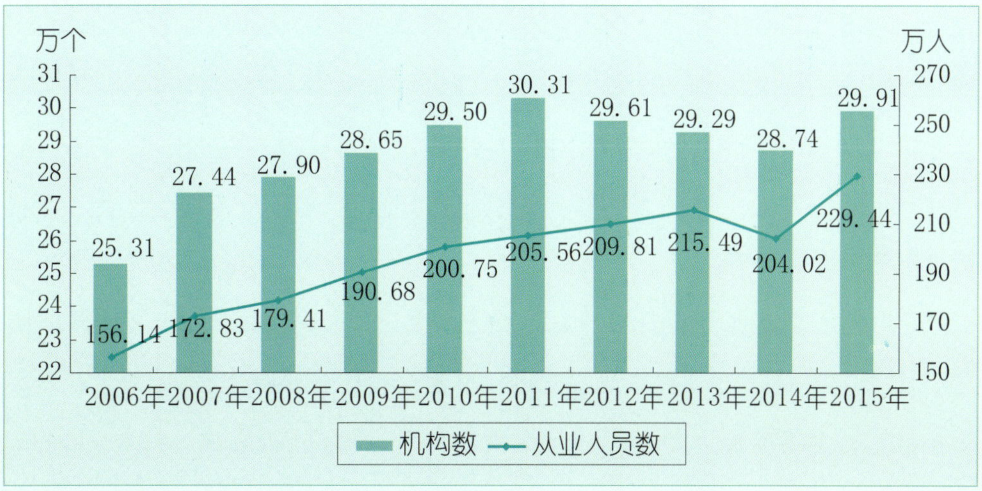

二、艺术创作演出

2015 年，艺术扶持政策措施更加完善。积极推动出台《关于支持戏曲传承发展的若干政策》，启动全国地方戏曲剧种普查，扶持“三个一批”戏曲剧本 27 个、“名家传戏”师徒 141 组。实施中国民族音乐舞蹈扶持发展工程，扶持“一带一路”主题采风创作项目 16 个。组织直属艺术单位 186 批、近 4400 人次文艺工作者深入基层，开展创作采风、结对帮扶、慰问演出等活动。国家艺术基金 2015 年立项资助 728 个项目。

年末全国共有艺术表演团体[4]10787 个，比上年末增加 2018 个，从业人员 30.18 万人，增加 3.90 万人。其中各级文化部门所属的艺术表演团体 2037 个，占 18.9%，从业人员 11.54 万人，占 38.2%。

全年全国艺术表演团体共演出 210.78 万场，比上年增长 21.2%，其中赴农村演出 139.08 万场，增长 21.9%，赴农村演出场次占总演出场次的 66.0%，比重比上年提高 0.4 个百分点；国内观众 9.58 亿人次，增长 5.3%，其中农村观众 5.85 亿人次，比上年增长 4.6%；总收入 257.65 亿元，比上年增长 13.8%，其中演出收入 93.93 亿元，增长 24.1%。

表 1　2007 年 –2015 年全国艺术表演团体基本情况

年　份	机构数（个）	从业人员数（人）	演出场次（万场）	国内演出观众人次（万人次）	总收入（万元）	
						#演出收入
2007 年	4512	220653	92.7	75895.6	829045	203757
2008 年	5114	208174	90.5	63186.8	933685	204842
2009 年	6139	184678	120.2	81715.9	1121559	288214
2010 年	6864	185413	137.1	88455.8	1239255	342696
2011 年	7055	226599	154.7	74585.1	1540263	526745
2012 年	7321	242047	135.0	82805.1	1968802	641480
2013 年	8180	260865	165.1	90064.3	2800266	820738
2014 年	8769	262887	173.9	91019.7	2264046	757028
2015 年	10787	301840	210.8	95799.0	2576483	939313

全年全国文化部门所属艺术表演团体共组织政府采购公益演出 13.87 万场，比上年增长 27.8%；观众 1.22 亿人次，增长 23.1%。利用流动舞台车演出 11.71 万场次，增长 10.3%；观众 10661.15 万人次，增长 7.7%。

年末全国共有艺术表演场馆 2143 个，观众坐席数 178.67 万个。各级文化部门所属艺术表演场馆 1264 个，比上年增加 16 个，观众坐席数 89.90 万个，比上年减少 2.08 万个；全年共举行艺术演出 5.45 万场次，比上年增长 7.3%；艺术演出观众人次 2388.11 万人次，增长 11.3%。

年末全国共有国有美术馆 408 个，比上年末增加 44 个，从业人员 3978 人，增加 404 人。全年共举办展览 5121 次，比上年增长 7.2%，参观人次 3053 万人次，增长 6.7%。

三、公共文化服务体系

2015 年，文化部通过完善顶层设计，切实推进基本公共文化服务标准化均等化。积极推动出台《关于加快构建现代公共文化服务体系的意见》、《关于推进基层综合性文化服务中心建设的指导意见》和《“十三五”时期贫困地区公共文化服务体系建设规划纲要》等文件，为全国公共文化事业的发展提供了有力保障。推动出台《关于做好政府向社会力量购买公共文化服务工作的意见》，引导社会力量参与公共文化服务体系建设。

（一）公共图书馆 [5]

年末全国共有公共图书馆 3139 个，比上年末增加 22 个。其中少儿图书馆 113 个，增加 5 个。年末全国公共图书馆从业人员 56422 人，比上年末增加 351 人。其中具有高级职称的人员 5746 人，占 10.2%；具有中级职称的人员 18475 人，占 32.7%。

年末全国公共图书馆实际使用房屋建筑面积 1316.76 万平方米，比上年末增长 6.9%；图书总藏量 [6]83844 万册，增长 6.0%，其中古籍 2712 万册；电子图书 83041 万册，增长 63.9%；阅览室座席数 91.07 万个，增长 6.5%；计算机 21.18 万台，增长 6.6%；供读者使用的电子阅览终端 12.67 万台，增长 4.2%。

年末全国平均每万人公共图书馆建筑面积 95.8 平方米，比上年末增加 5.8 平方米；全国人均图书藏量 0.61 册，增加 0.03 册；全年全国人均购书费 1.43 元，比上年增加 0.19 元。

图 2　2006 年 –2015 年全国公共图书馆人均资源情况

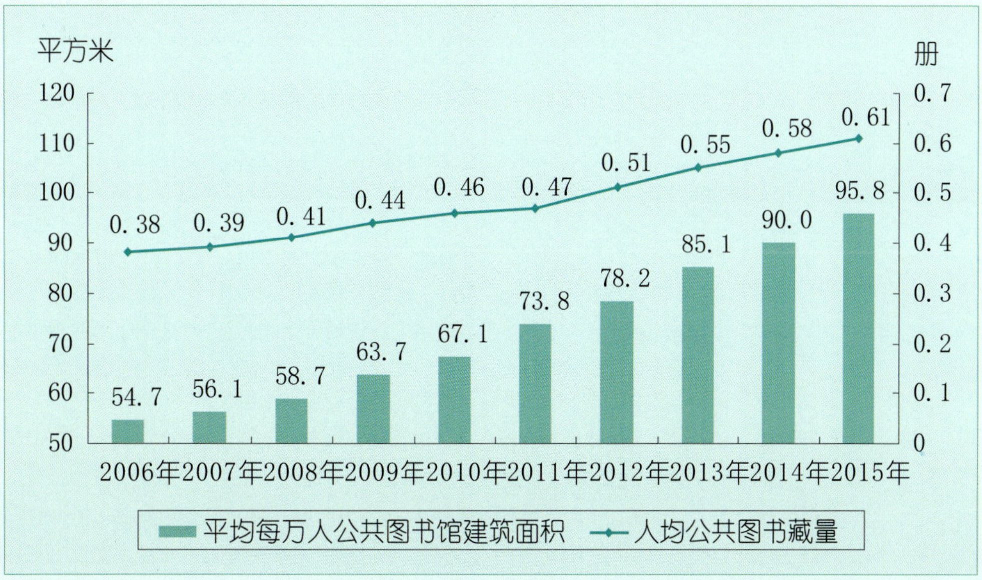

全年全国公共图书馆发放借书证[7]5721 万个，比上年增长 45.1%；总流通人次[8]58892 万，增长 11.0%。书刊文献外借册次 50896 万，增长 8.9%；外借人次 23085 万，增长 1.5%。全年共为读者举办各种活动 114544 次，增长 10.6%；参加人次 5908 万，增长 17.8%。

图 3　2006 年 –2015 年全国公共图书馆总流通人次及书刊外借册次

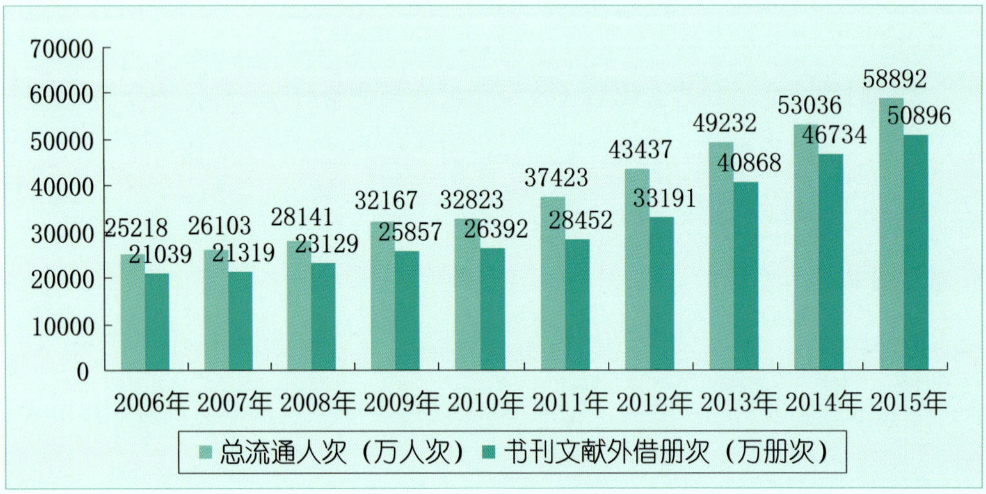

（二）群众文化机构[9]

年末全国共有群众文化机构 44291 个，比上年末减少 132 个。其中乡镇综合文化站 34239 个，减少 226 个。年末全国群众文化机构从业人员 173499 人，比上年末增加 3200 人。其中具有高级职称的人员 5893 人，占 3.4%；具有中级职称的人员 16898 人，占 9.7%。

年末全国群众文化机构实际使用房屋建筑面积 3848.27 万平方米，比上年末增长 4.4%；藏书 2.62 亿册，增长 5.6%；计算机 36.14 万台，增长 4.2%；对公众开放的阅览室 109.23 万平方米，增长 1.1%。年末全国平均每万人群众文化设施建筑面积 279.95 平方米，比上年末提高 10.44 平方米。

图 4　2006 年 –2015 年全国平均每万人群众文化设施建筑面积

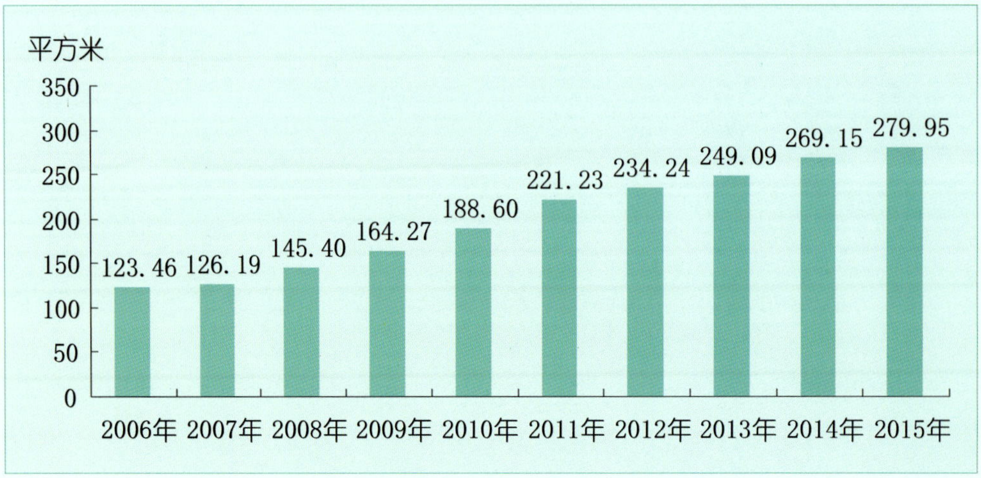

全年全国群众文化机构共组织开展各类文化活动[10]166.39 万场次，比上年增长 13.0%；服务人次 54827 万，增长 8.2%。

表 2 2015 年全国群众文化机构开展活动情况

项 目	总量		比上年增长（%）	
	活动次数（万次）	服务人次（万人次）	活动次数	服务人次
各项活动总计	166.39	54827	13.0	8.2
其中：展览	13.98	10752	6.2	4.8
文艺活动	95.99	39728	13.5	9.2
公益性讲座	2.79	478	9.0	7.4
训练班	53.63	3868	14.3	8.1

年末全国群众文化机构共有馆办文艺团体[11]7618 个，演出 15.23 万场，观众 8430 万人次。由文化馆（站）指导的群众业余文艺团体 38.32 万个，馆办老年大学 853 个。

四、文化市场

年末全国文化市场经营单位[12]23.17 万家，比上年末增加 1.15 万家；从业人员 156.47 万人，增加 24.08 万人。全年全国文化市场经营单位营业总收入 2965.64 亿元，营业利润 1002.10 亿元。

分区域看，年末城市文化市场经营单位 83598 个，占文化市场经营单位总量的 36.1%；县城 93228 个，占 40.2%；县以下地区 54883 个，占 23.7%。

表 3 2015 年按区域全国文化市场经营单位主要指标

		机构数（个）	从业人员数（人）	营业总收入（万元）	营业利润（万元）
总量	总计	231709	1564660	29656346	10020910
	城市	83598	720371	22838853	7965993
	县城	93228	653781	5356224	1616637
	县以下	54883	190508	1461269	438280
比重（%）	总计	100.0	100.0	100.0	100.0
	城市	36.1	46.0	77.0	79.5
	县城	40.2	41.8	18.1	16.1
	县以下	23.7	12.2	4.9	4.4

年末全国共有娱乐场所 79816 个，从业人员 67.36 万人，全年营业总收入 557.04 亿元，营业利润 136.17 亿元。

年末全国共有互联网上网服务营业场所 134847 个，从业人员 48.03 万人，全年营业总收入 400.97 亿元，营业利润 130.30 亿元。

五、文化产业与文化科技

2015 年，文化部推进国家文化产业创新实验区建设，开展拉动城乡居民文化消费试点项目，积极探索建立扩大文化消费长效机制。推动落实国务院关于推进文化创意和设计服务与相关产业融合发展的政策措施，实施文化产业创业创意人才扶持计划。推动将特色文化产业发展纳入中央财政文化产业发展专项资金重点支持范围，支持专项资金 1.66 亿元。落实《藏羌彝文化产业走廊总体规划》，推进藏羌彝等民族聚居地区文化与生态、旅游的融合发展。扶持成长型小微文化企业发展。深化文化金融合作，联合财政部实施“文化金融扶持计划”，对 138 个重点项目给予 11.8 亿元资金支持，同比增长 75%。截至 2015 年末，累计带动 8330 亿元的金融资本，超 1.8 万亿元的社会资本投入文化产业。建设国家文化产业项目服务平台，为优秀文化产业项目提供公共服务，截至 2015 年末，共征集 7134 个文化产业项目。

年末全国共有 10 个国家级文化产业示范园区，10 个国家级文化产业试验园区和 335 个国家文化产业示范基地。

2015 年，60 个动漫项目入选弘扬社会主义核心价值观动漫扶持计划，46 个动漫项目入选国家动漫品牌建设和保护计划。加强对优秀原创动漫作品的宣传推广，提高动漫会展专业化、市场化水平。促进动漫与新媒体渠道对接，助推互联网 + 动漫发展，推进数字内容产业发展。在国际电信联盟推出中国自主原创的手机动漫标准，抢占国际标准制定权。年末经文化部、财政部、国家税务总局三部门联合认定的动漫企业共有 730 个，重点动漫企业 43 个。

2015 年，文化部积极推动科技项目组织实施与成果应用，53 个项目获批为国家科技支撑计划项目、国家文化科技提升计划项目、国家标准化项目等，完成 47 项文化科技创新类项目的验收结项工作。加强项目管理，遴选培育对策性、时代性、创新性俱佳的艺术科研项目，4 个项目确立为国家社科基金艺术学重大项目，184 个项目确立为国家社科基金艺术学年度项目，71 个项目确立为文化部文化艺术科学研究项目。完成 127 项全国艺术科学规划项目的鉴定结项工作。

六、文化遗产保护

国家文物局实施 40 个抗战类国保单位维修项目，113 处抗战类全国重点文物保护单位全部对外开放。首批 51 个传统村落保护工程全面完工，启动第二批 100 个传统村落保护利用项目。“平安故宫”

工程、中共六大会址修复工程扎实推进。2015 年 7 月，“中国土司遗址”成功列入《世界文化遗产名录》，至此我国拥有 48 处世界遗产，位居世界第二。

年末全国共有文物机构 8676 个，比上年末增加 255 个。其中，文物保护管理机构 3307 个，占 38.1%，博物馆[13]3852 个，占 44.4%。年末全国文物机构从业人员 14.60 万人，比上年末减少 0.21 万人。其中高级职称 8000 人，占 5.5%，中级职称 18313 人，占 12.5%。

图 5　2006 年 –2015 年全国文物单位机构数及从业人员数

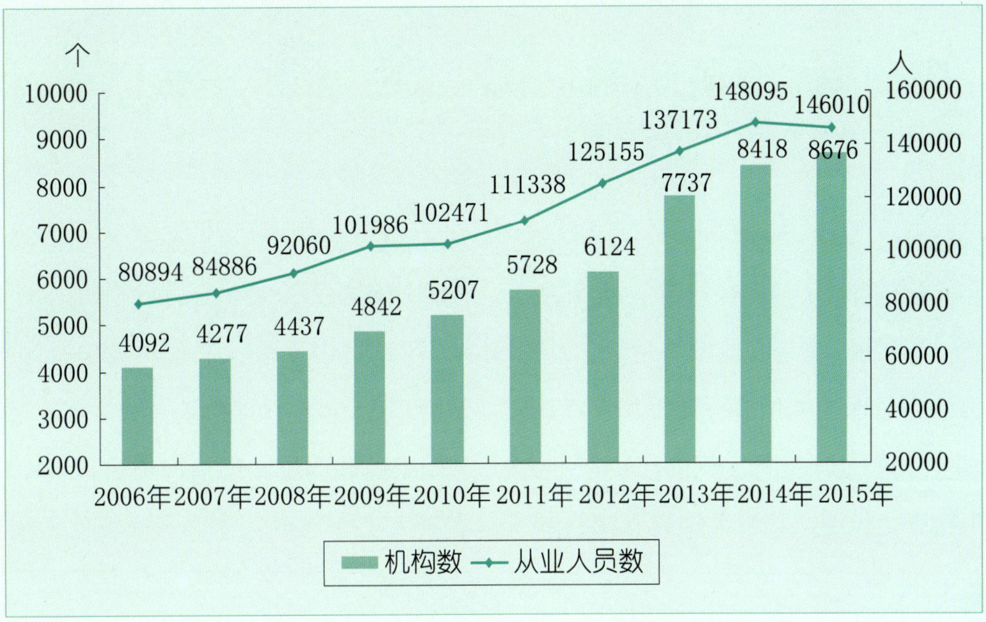

年末全国文物机构拥有文物藏品 4139.19 万件，比上年末增加 75.61 万件，增长 1.9%。其中，博物馆文物藏品 3044.14 万件，占文物藏品总量的 73.5%；文物商店文物藏品 728.02 万件，占 17.6%。文物藏品中，一级文物 10.87 万件，占 0.3%；二级文物 71.54 万件，占 1.7%；三级文物 388.80 万件，占 9.4%。年末全国不可移动文物共有 76.67 万件。

全年全国文物机构共安排基本陈列[14]10859 个，举办临时展览[15]11805 个，接待观众 92508 万人次，比上年增长 9.8%。其中未成年人 24663 万人次，增长 10.1%，占参观总人数的 26.7%。博物馆接待观众 78112 万人次，增长 8.8%，占文物机构接待观众 84.4%。

图 6　2008 年 –2015 年全国文物机构接待观众人次及未成年人观众人次

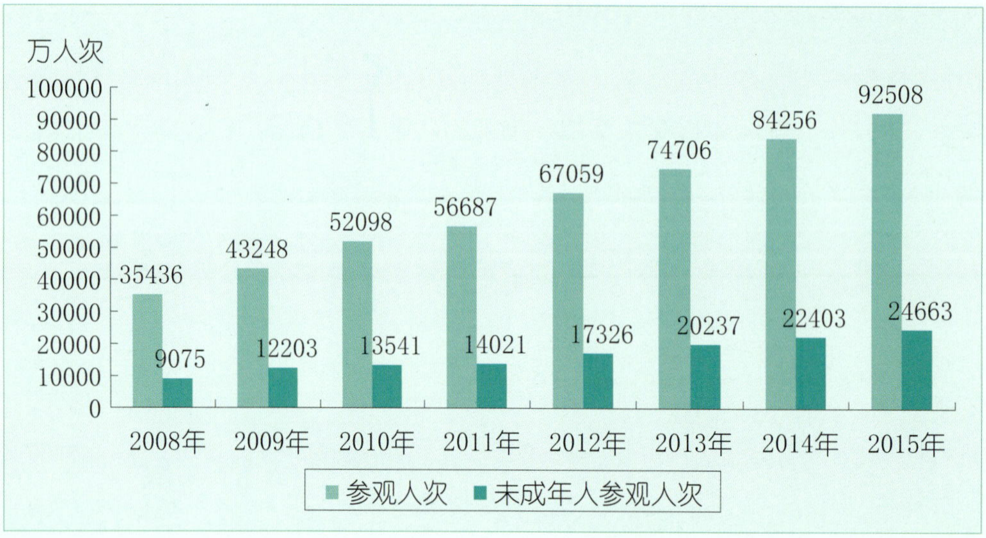

2015 年，文化部制定《国家级非物质文化遗产代表性传承人抢救性记录工作规范》，支持 268 位国家级非遗代表性传承人的抢救性记录。认定 464 家第四批国家级非遗代表性项目保护单位，对 331 家不适合的项目保护单位进行调整和重新认定。截至 2015 年末，国务院共公布了 1372 个国家级非物质文化遗产代表性项目，文化部共认定了 1986 名国家级非物质文化遗产项目代表性传承人。我国有 30 项非物质文化遗产项目入选联合国教科文组织“人类非物质文化遗产代表作名录”、7 项入选“急需保护的非物质文化遗产名录”，1 项入选“优秀实践名册”，总数位列世界第一。据初步统计，年末全国共有非物质文化遗产保护机构[16]2637 个，从业人员 18657 人。全年全国非物质文化遗产保护机构共举办展览 16937 次，比上年增长 5.6%，接待观众 3297 万人次，比上年降低 2.7%；举办演出 39161 场，观众 3958 万人次，分别比上年增长 12.8% 和 4.3%；举办民俗活动 13567 次，比上年增长 4.5%，观众 3717 万人次，比上年降低 4.3%；举办培训班 20588 次，比上年降低 1.7%，培训人数 151 万人次，比上年增长 10.2%。

七、对外和对港澳台文化交流

2015 年，文化部服务国家“一带一路”战略，举办第十四届亚洲艺术节暨第二届海上丝绸之路国际艺术节、“东亚文化之都”、中国－中东欧国家文化合作论坛等活动。举办中加、中英文化交流年、中美文化论坛、中俄文化大集、南非中国文化年、赫尔辛基艺术节中国主宾国等重点文化外交活动。积极参与高级别人文交流机制以及政府间对话活动，有力配合国家外交大局。

推动地方政府与企业参与海外中国文化中心建设，2015 年 5 家海外中国文化中心投入运营，总数达到 25 个。据统计，25 个海外文化中心全年共举办培训班 221 次，培训 16035 人次；举办讲座 197 次，参加 16147 人次；组织各类文化活动 924 次，参加 280.14 万人次。“欢乐春节”活动以“品牌化、本土化、市场化”为宗旨，在全球 119 个国家和地区开展 900 多项文化活动。北京、上海、深圳国家对外文化贸易基地的影响力和辐射带动作用进一步显现。

深化职能转变，调整台湾来大陆文化交流项目审批权限。成功举办港澳大学生文化实践活动、“粤港澳青年文化之旅”、“艺海流金——丝路寻根之旅”、“情系丝路——牵手宁夏”、“两岸文学对话”等活动，为两岸暨港澳台地区青年搭建交流平台，提升思想领域深度交流。举办“根与魂”非遗展演、庆春节、庆中秋等活动，入岛举办北京文化庙会等，共同促进中华文化传承发展，发挥文化交流在促进人心回归、凝聚亲情方面的长效作用。

全年经文化系统审批的对外文化交流项目 1667 起，40781 人次参加；对港澳文化交流项目 230 项，5593 人次参加；对台文化交流项目 500 项，12593 人次参加。

八、文化资金投入

2015 年，中央财政通过继续实施“三馆一站”免费开放、非物质文化遗产保护、公共数字文化建设、地市级公共文化设施建设等文化项目，共落实中央补助地方专项资金 47.80 亿元，比上年增长 2.7%。

图 7　2006 年 –2015 年中央对地方文化项目补助资金情况

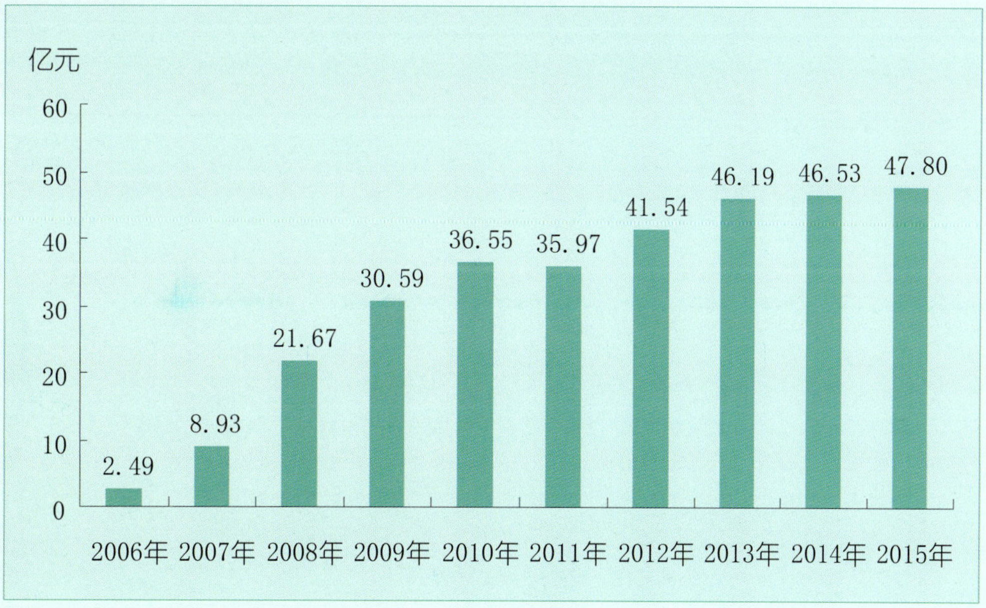

全年全国文化事业费[17]682.97 亿元，比上年增加 99.53 亿元，增长 17.1%，增长速度比上年提高 7.1 个百分点；全国人均文化事业费 49.68 元，比上年增加 7.03 元，增长 16.5%。

图 8　2006 年 –2015 年全国人均文化事业费及增长速度

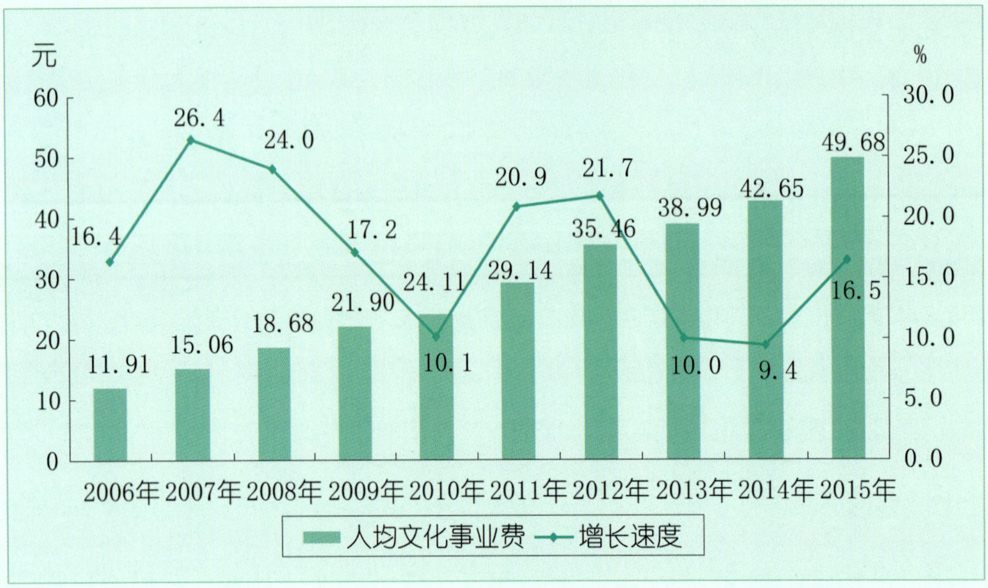

文化事业费占财政总支出的比重为 0.39%，比重比上年提高 0.01 个百分点。

图 9　全国文化事业费占财政总支出比重

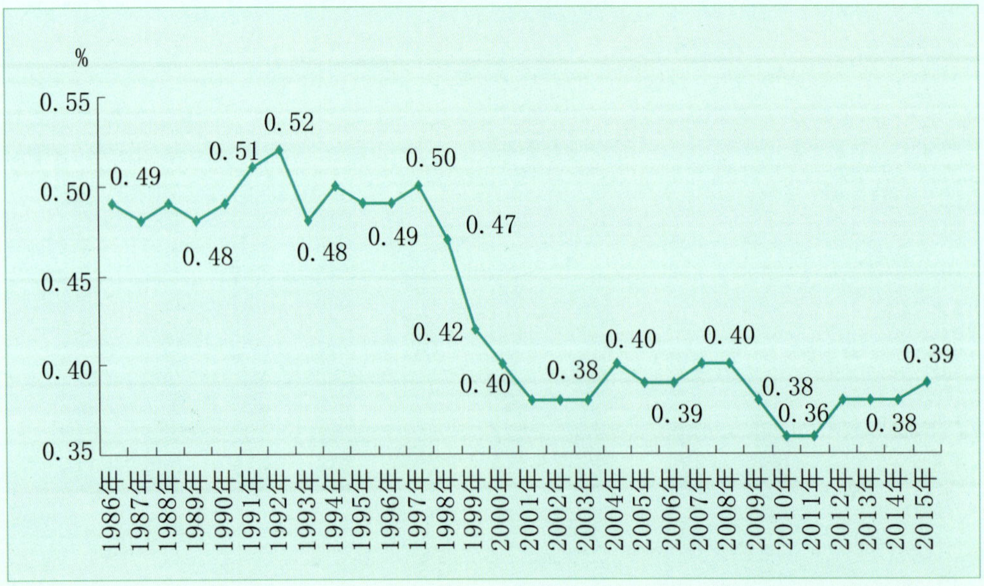

全国文化事业费中，县以上文化单位 352.84 亿元，占 51.7%，比重比上年提高了 1.6 个百分点；县及县以下文化单位 330.13 亿元，占 48.3%，比重比上年下降了 1.6 个百分点。东部地区[18]文化单位文化事业费 287.87 亿元，占 42.1%，比重提高了 0.5 个百分点；中部地区文化单位 164.27 亿元，占 24.1%，比重提高了 1.2 个百分点；西部地区文化单位 193.87 亿元，占 28.4%，比重下降了 0.9 个百分点。

表 4 全国文化事业费按城乡和区域分布情况

项目		1995 年	2000 年	2005 年	2010 年	2013 年	2014 年	2015 年
总量（亿元）	全国	33.39	63.16	133.82	323.06	530.49	583.44	682.97
	#县以上	24.44	46.33	98.12	206.65	272.67	292.12	352.84
	县及县以下	8.95	16.87	35.70	116.41	257.82	291.32	330.13
	#东部地区	13.43	28.85	64.37	143.35	231.41	242.98	287.87
	中部地区	9.54	15.05	30.58	78.65	120.01	133.46	164.27
	西部地区	8.30	13.70	27.56	85.78	152.16	171.15	193.87
所占比重（%）	全国	100.0	100.0	100.0	100.0	100.0	100.0	100.0
	#县以上	73.2	73.4	73.3	64.0	51.4	50.1	51.7
	县及县以下	26.8	26.7	26.7	36.0	48.6	49.9	48.3
	#东部地区	40.2	45.7	48.1	44.4	43.6	41.6	42.1
	中部地区	28.6	23.8	22.9	24.3	22.6	22.9	24.1
	西部地区	24.9	21.7	20.6	26.6	28.7	29.3	28.4

全年全国文物事业费[19]280.37 亿元，比上年增加 32.50 亿元，增长 13.1%；文物事业费占财政总支出的比重为 0.16%，比重比上年减少 0.01 个百分点。

据财政部统计，2015 年全国财政支出中，文化体育传媒经费[20]3067 亿元，比上年增长 14.0%，占财政支出的 1.74%，比重比上年下降 0.03 个百分点。

图 10 2006 年 –2015 年全国文化体育传媒经费总量及增长速度

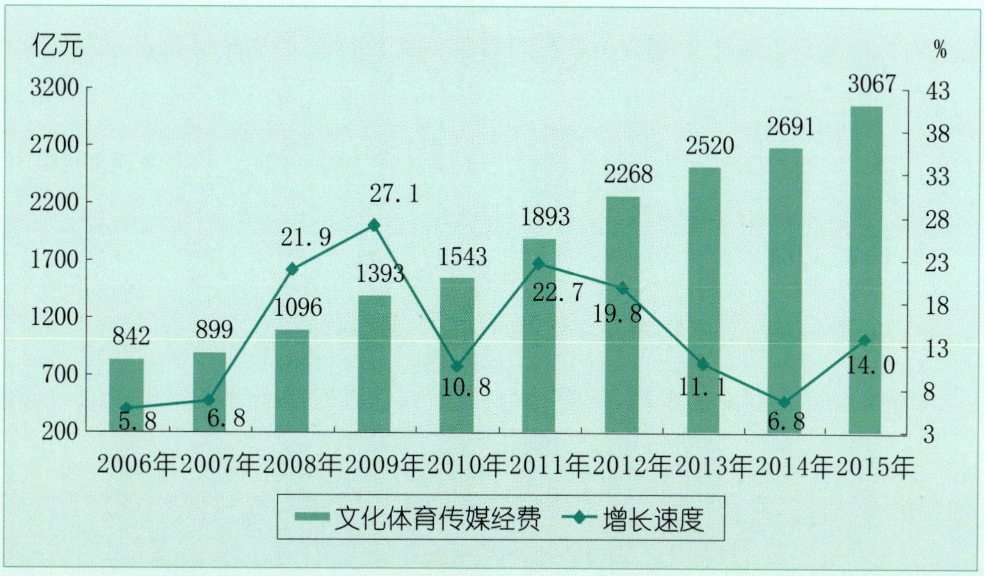

注释：

[1] 本公报中各项数据为初步统计数据。各项统计数据均未包括香港特别行政区、澳门特别行政区和台湾省。部分数据因四舍五入的原因，存在着与分项合计不等的情况。

[2] 文化单位是指全国各级文化部门（含文化系统和文物系统）主办的或实行行业管理的文化机构，不含各级新闻出版、广播影视等部门主办或管理的文化机构。根据现行的统计制度，文化部门主办的文化单位（如公共图书馆、文化馆、文化站、博物馆、公有制艺术表演团体、公有制艺术表演场馆等）全部纳入了统计范围，实行行业管理的文化单位中，娱乐场所和互联网上网服务营业场所、非公有制艺术表演团体、非公有制艺术表演场馆、经营性互联网文化单位、艺术品经营机构和演出经纪机构均纳入统计。

[3] 从业人员是指在各级文化部门（含文化系统和文物系统）主办或实行行业管理的机构中工作并取得劳动报酬的人员。统计范围同文化单位。

[4] 艺术表演团体指由文化部门主办或实行行业管理（经文化行政部门审批并领取营业性演出许可证），专门从事表演艺术等活动的各类专业艺术表演团体。

[5] 公共图书馆是指由各级文化部门主办的、面向社会公众开放并提供科学、文化等各种知识普及教育的机构。

[6] 公共图书馆总藏量指已编目的古籍、图书、期刊和报纸的合订本、手册、手稿，以及缩微制品、录像带、录音带、光盘等视听文献资料数量之和，不包括电子图书。

[7] 公共图书馆发放的借书证数是指由公共图书馆发放，并在当年内使用过至少一次的借书证数。

[8] 公共图书馆总流通人次是指本年度内到图书馆场馆接受图书馆服务的总人次，包括借阅书刊、咨询问题，以及参加各类读者活动等。

[9] 群众文化机构是指各级文化部门主办的开展群众文化活动的场所，主要包括文化馆（含综合性文化中心、群众艺术馆）、文化站。

[10] 群众文化机构组织开展活动是指组织文艺活动、举办训练班、举办展览和组织公益性讲座总和。

[11] 群众文化机构馆办文艺团体指由本馆人员组成的为群众提供文艺演出的演出团队。

[12] 文化市场经营单位指经文化市场行政部门审批或备案并领取相关许可或备案文件的、从事文化经营和文化服务活动的机构。按照现行统计制度，文化市场经营单位统计范围包括娱乐场所和互联网上网服务营业场所、非公有制艺术表演团体、非公有制艺术表演场馆、经营性互联网文化单位、艺术品经营机构和演出经纪机构。

[13] 博物馆指为了研究、教育、欣赏的目的，收藏、保护、展示人类活动和自然环境的见证物，

向公众开放，非营利性、永久性社会服务机构，包括以博物馆（院）、纪念馆（舍）、科技馆、陈列馆等专有名称开展活动的单位。

[14] 基本陈列指在本馆布置陈列、地点固定、时间较长的展出。

[15] 临时展览指在本机构内设置，由本馆设计布陈，形式比较多样的展出。

[16] 非物质文化遗产保护机构是指各级非物质文化遗产保护中心或非物质文化遗产保护办公室。

[17] 文化事业费是指区域内各级财政对文化系统主办单位的经费投入总和。一般包括艺术表演团体、公共图书馆、文化馆（站）等文化事业单位的财政拨款（不含基建拨款）及文化部门所属企业的财政补贴。根据现行统计口径，文化事业费不包括各级文化行政管理部门的行政运行经费。

[18] 东部地区包括北京、天津、辽宁、上海、江苏、浙江、福建、山东、广东；中部地区包括河北、山西、吉林、黑龙江、安徽、江西、河南、湖北、湖南、海南；西部地区包括内蒙古、广西、重庆、四川、贵州、云南、西藏、陕西、甘肃、青海、宁夏、新疆。

[19] 文物事业费是指区域内各级财政对文物事业的经费投入总和。一般包括博物馆、文物保护管理机构等文物事业单位的财政拨款（不含基建拨款）及文物部门所属企业的财政补贴。

[20] 文化体育传媒经费数据源自财政部，是指各级政府在文化、文物、体育、广播影视和新闻出版方面的投入。

Statistical Communiqué of the Ministry of Culture of the People's Republic of China on Cultural Development in 2015[1]

In 2015, all official cultural departments in China have implemented and put into practice the the guiding principles from the 18th CPC National Congress, the 3rd, 4th and the 5th Plenary Sessions of the 18th CPC Central Committee, and General Secretary Xi Jinping's major policy addresses, and worked in accordance with the overall plan for promoting all-round economic, political, cultural, social, and ecological progress. With the aim to further promote the advanced socialist culture, they put people at the center of their work, made new achievements in cultural reform and development and accomplished various tasks stipulated in the 12th Five Year Plan with a progressive and innovative approach. Their work laid a solid cultural foundation for the cause of building a culturally strong socialist China and a all-round well-off society, and achieving the Chinese Dream of the rejuvenation of the Chinese nation.

I. Institution and Employment

299,100 national cultural units[2] were brought into statistical range by the end of 2015, 11,700 more than that of the previous year; the number of employees[3] was 2.2944 million, 254.2 thousand persons more than the previous year. Among them, 65,714 units were affiliated to government cultural departments, 152 more than those of the past year, with 645,300 employees, 7,124 persons more than those of the previous year.

Figure 1: Number of national cultural units and employed persons in 2006-2015

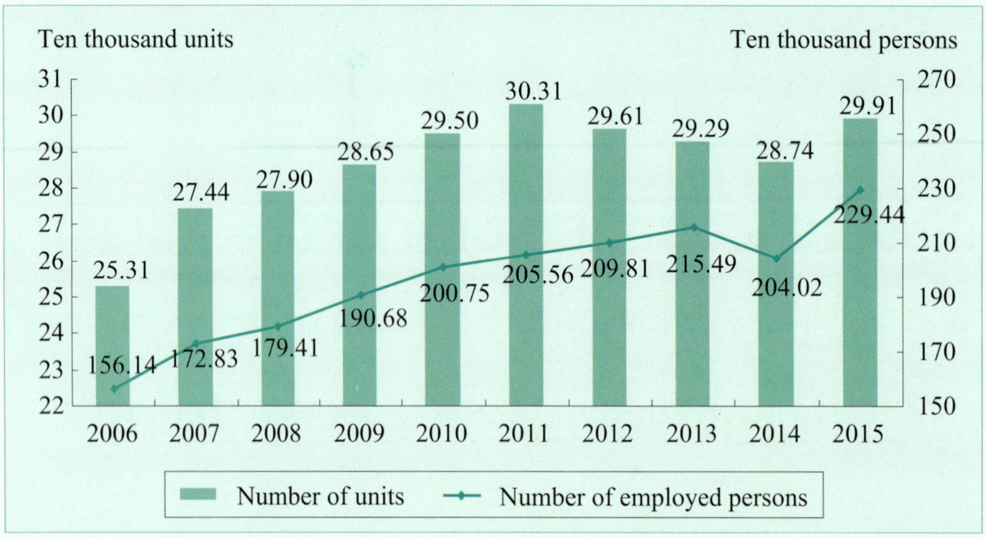

II. Performing Arts

In 2015, policies and measures to support arts growth have been improved. The Ministry of Culture of China enacted Several Policies to Support Traditional Chinese Operas, launched the national census for local traditional opera genres, and gave financial support to 27 significant plays identified by the Ministry which were either original, or adapted from foreign operas, or rearranged into a newer form, and 141 groups of opera masters and students to encourage renowned arts masters to pass on their skill. A project to facilitate the development of folk music and dance was initiated which provided support to 16 artistic field trip programs with the theme of the Belt and Road Initiative. 186 teams with about 4,400 artists from art institutions affiliated to government cultural departments have been send to the grassroots for field trips, providing cultural and arts aids to their local counterparts, and giving special artistic showcases. The National Arts Fund of China provided financial support to 728 arts programs in 2015.

By the end of the year, the number of art performance troupes[4] reached 10,787, an increase of 2,018 over the end of the previous year; that of the professionals reached 301,800 with the increase of 39,000. Of them, the art performance troupes managed by cultural departments at all levels reached 2,037, accounting for 18.9% of the total with 115,400 art employees, which is 38.2% of the total.

In 2014, all art troupes in China presented 2.1078 million performances, an increase of 21.2% over the previous year; the domestic audiences reached 958 million, up by 5.3%; the number of performances for rural areas was 1.3908 million, up by 22%, accounting for 66% of the total, 0.4 percentage points higher than that of the previous year; that of the rural audiences was 585 million, up by 4.6% than that of the previous year. The total turnover of the performing troupes was 25.765 billion yuan, an increase of 13.8% over the previous year; of them the income from performing arts was 9.393 billion yuan, up by 24.1%.

Table 1: General information of art troupes nationwide in 2007-2015

Year	Number of institutions	Number of employees	Number of shows (ten thousand)	Number of domestic audience attendances (ten thousand)	Total income (ten thousand yuan)	
						#Shows' box office
2007	4512	220653	92.7	75895.6	829045	203757
2008	5114	208174	90.5	63186.8	933685	204842
2009	6139	184678	120.2	81715.9	1121559	288214
2010	6864	185413	137.1	88455.8	1239255	342696
2011	7055	226599	154.7	74585.1	1540263	526745
2012	7321	242047	135.0	82805.1	1968802	641480
2013	8180	260865	165.1	90064.3	2800266	820738
2014	8769	262887	173.9	91019.7	2264046	757028
2015	10787	301840	210.8	95799.0	2576483	939313

The amount of government-purchased public performances presented by art performance troupes affiliated to official cultural departments throughout the year was 138,700, 27.8% increase over the number of the previous year, with audiences of 122 million, up by 23.1%. The number of the performances on traveling stage vans was 117,100, up by 10.3%, with audience attendances of 106.6115 million, up by 7.7%.

By the end of the year, the venues of the performing arts amounted to 2,143, with 1,786,700 seats. Among them, 1,264 are state-owned (16 venues more than those of the last year) with 899,000 seats in total (20,800 seats less than those of last year). 54,500 performances were held throughout the year, up by 7.3% over the previous year; the audiences reached 23.8811 million, an increase of 11.3%.

By the end of 2015, there were 408 art museums in China, 44 more than those of the previous year, with 3,978 employees, 404 more than the previous year. 5,121 exhibitions were presented by these museums year-round, attracting 30.53 million visitor attendances, up by 7.2% and 6.7% over those of the previous year respectively.

III. Public Cultural Service System

In 2015, the Ministry of Culture improved the top-tier design for substantially drive forward the standardization and equal accessibility of basic public cultural services. Promulgation of the Opinions on Accelerating the Building of A Modern Public Cultural Services System, the Guild Lines to Promote Comprehensive Cultural Service Centers on Grassroot Level and the Plan on Public Cultural Service System Development in Poverty-stricken Areas during the 13th Five-Year-Plan Period were actively accelerated, which provided substantial support for the growth of public cultural undertakings in China. The release of Opinions on Encouraging Governmental Purchase of Public Cultural Services was also facilitated to engage more social sectors in developing an accomplished public cultural service system.

(1) Public Libraries[5]

By the end of the year, there were in total 3,139 libraries nationwide, 22 more than the number of the previous year. Among them, children's libraries were 113, an increase of 5. The total number of employees of public libraries across China reached 56,422, 351 more than the number of the previous year. Among them, 5,746 owned senior professional titles, accounting for 10.2%, and 18,475 owned medium-level professional titles, accounting for 32.7%.

According to statistics at the end of 2015, the actual floor space used by public library buildings totaled 13.1676 million m^2, up by 6.9% over the end of the previous year. 838.44 million books[6] (among them 2,172 are ancient books) and 830.41 million E-books were collected in these libraries, up by 6.0% and 63.9% respectively. The number of seats in reading rooms was 910,700, up by 6.5%, and that of computers was 211,800, up by 6.6%, and that of electronic reading terminals for readers was 126,700, up by 4.2%.

By the end of the 2015 the floor space of public libraries for each ten thousand persons was 95.8 m^2, an increase of 5.8 m^2 over the end of the previous year; the number of books per capita was 0.61, an increase of 0.03 over the previous year; the money spent on books per capita was 1.43 yuan, an increase of 0.19 yuan over previous year.

Figure 2: Information of per capita resource of national public libraries in 2006-2015

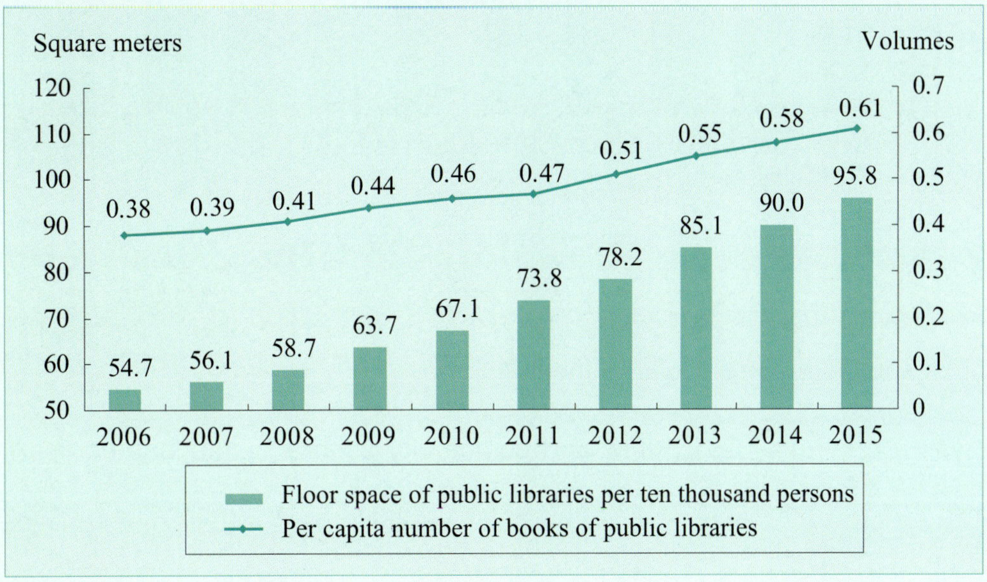

The library cards[7] issued by public public libraries across the country throughout the year total to 57.21 million, up by 45.1% since the previous year; the total flow of person-time[8] reached 588.92 million, a growth of 11.0%. The total circulation number of books, magazines, and documents loaned to library users reached 508.96 million, up by 8.9%; a total of 230.85 million people borrowed books, a growth of 1.5%. Various activities organized for readers total to 114,544, up by 10.6%; which attracted 59.08 million person-times, an increase of 17.8%.

Figure 3: Total flow of person-time and number of books lent out of national public libraries in 2006-2015

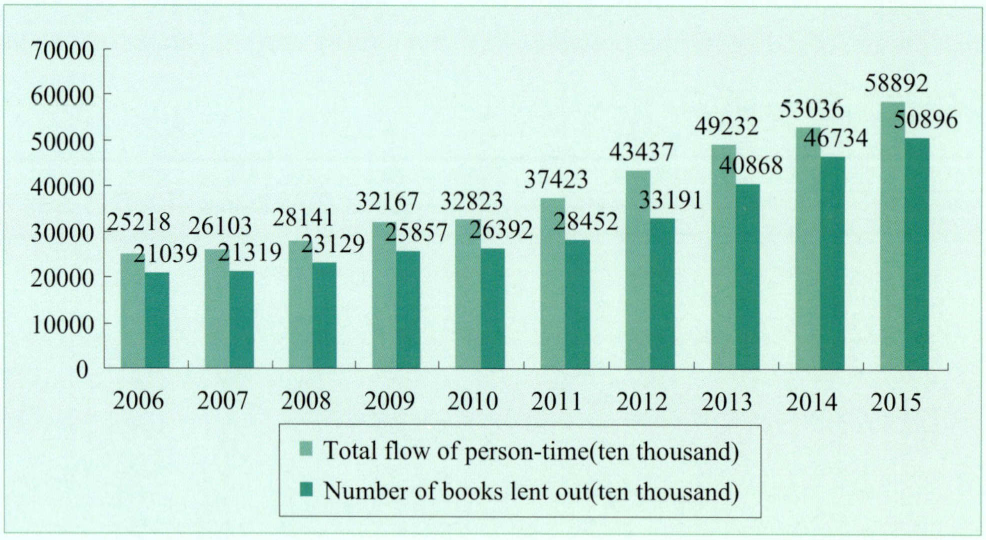

(2) Public and Community Cultural Institutions[9]

There was a total of 44,291 public and community cultural institutions across the country by the end of 2015, a decrease of 132 since the previous year. Among these, township-level comprehensive cultural stations reached a total of 34,239, a decrease of 226. By the end of the year, the total employees of public and community cultural institutions nationwide reached 173,499, an increase of 3,200 since the previous year. Staff with senior professional titles reached 5,893, accounting for 3.4%; and staffs with medium-grade professional titles reached 16,898, accounting for 9.7%.

By the end of the year, the actual floor space used by public and community institutions was 38,482,700, up by 4.4% since the previous year; the number of book collections reached 262 million, up by 5.6%; total computers reached 361,400, up by 4.2%; public reading rooms areas covered a total of 1.0923 million m^2, up by 1.1%. By the end of the year, the area covered by cultural facilities for every ten thousand people reached 279.95 m^2, an increase of 10.44 m^2 since the previous year.

Figure 4: Floor space of national cultural facilities of mass per ten thousand people in 2006-2015

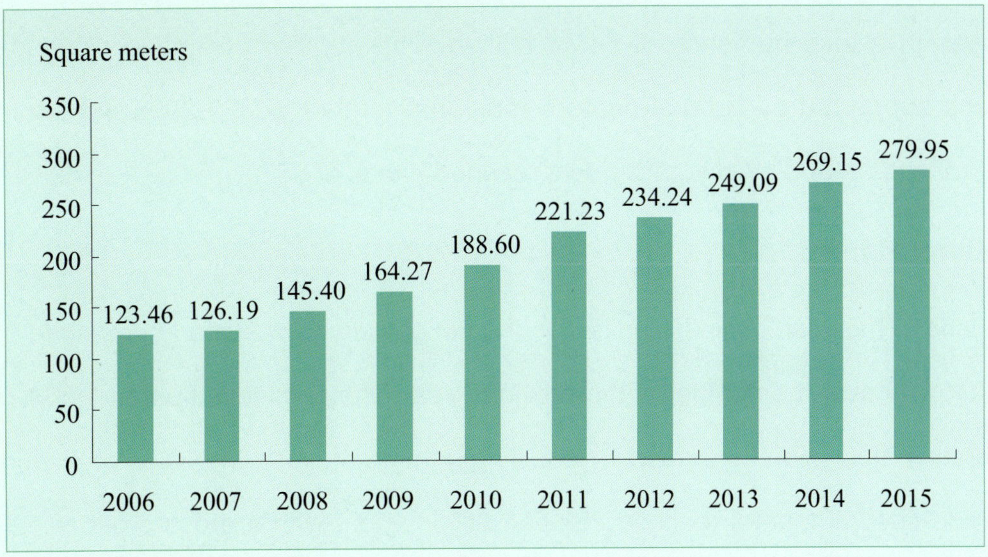

The number of activities[10] organized by nationwide public and community cultural institutions throughout the year reached 1,663,900, up by 13% since the previous year; total people served reached 548.27 million, up by 8.2%.

Table 2: Information of activities organized by nationwide public and community cultural institutions in 2015

	Gross		Increase over previous year (%)	
	Number of activity (ten thousand)	Number of participants (ten thousand person-time)	Number of activity	Person-time of participants
Aggregate of activities	**166.39**	**54827**	**13.0**	**8.2**
#Exhibition	13.98	10752	6.2	4.8
Cultural activities	95.99	39728	13.5	9.2
Public lecture	2.79	478	9.0	7.4
Training class	53.63	3868	14.3	8.1

By the end of the year, public and community cultural institutions nationwide fostered a total of 7,618 cultural and arts organizations [11] under cultural centers, which presented 152,300 performances to a total audience of 84.30 million. The number of amateur cultural and arts organizations supported by cultural centers (stations) totaled to 383,200, and senior citizen's community colleges set up by cultural centers reached a total of 853.

IV. Cultural Market

By the end of the year, business units[12] in the nationwide cultural market reached 231,700, an increase of 11,500 over the number of the previous year. They employed about 1,564,700 people, 240,800 persons more than the previous year. Throughout the year, the sales of business units in the nationwide cultural market reached 296.564 billion yuan, with a gross profit of 100.21 billion yuan.

By the end of the year, the number of business units in urban cultural markets was 83,598, accounting for 36.1% of the total operating units in the cultural market; there were 93,228 county-level business units, accounting for 40.2%; and 54,883 business units based in areas lower than county, accounting for 23.7%.

Table 3: Key indicators for business units in the national cultural market according to area in 2015

		Number of institutions	Employed people	Gross revenue (ten thousand yuan)	Gross profit (ten thousand yuan)
Amount	**Aggregate**	**231709**	**1564660**	**29656346**	**10020910**
	City	83598	720371	22838853	7965993
	County	93228	653781	5356224	1616637
	Areas lower than county-level	54883	190508	1461269	438280
Proportion (%)	**Aggregate**	**100.0**	**100.0**	**100.0**	**100.0**
	City	36.1	46.0	77.0	79.5
	County	40.2	41.8	18.1	16.1
	Areas lower than county-level	23.7	12.2	4.9	4.4

By the end of the year, the number of entertainment venues totaled 79,816, with the number of employees reaching 673,600; their annual business revenue amounted to 55.704 billion yuan, and their profit reached 13.617 billion yuan.

By the end of the year, internet access services had a total of 134,847 business sites across the country; the number of employed people reached 480,300; annual business income amounted to 40.097 billion yuan, with a profit of 13.03 billion yuan.

V. Cultural Industries and Related Technology

In 2015, the Ministry of Culture promoted the development of state-level cultural industry parks and bases, initiated pilot programs to spur cultural consumption for unban and rural consumers, and actively explored the possibilities to establish and enrich long-term mechanisms to increase cultural consumption. The Ministry also facilitated the implementation of policies and measures that encouraged the integrated growth of creativity, design and related industries, and launched the incentive program for business starters and creative workers in cultural industry.

The Ministry facilitated the inclusion of specialized cultural businesses' development into the coverage of the special fund for cultural industries of the central budget, and applied for 166 million yuan as targeted supportive fund. The Overall Plan for Cultural Industry Corridor in the Habitats of Tibetan, Qiang and Yi Ethnic Groups was implemented to promote the cultural, ecological and tourism development in these areas in an integrated way. The Ministry also supported the growth of sustainable cultural SMEs, and joined efforts with the Ministry of Finance to input 1.18 billion yuan into 138 key projects, 75% more than that of the previous year. By the end of 2015, the input has maneuvered 833 billion yuan's capital assets and 1800 billion yuan's investment from the private sectors to invest in cultural industry. The Ministry made efforts to build service platforms for national cultural industry projects to provide publicly accessible services to excellent creative projects. By the end of 2015, 7,134 projects have registered for such services.

By the end of 2015, there were in total 10 National Role Model Parks for Cultural Industry, 10 National Pilot Parks for Cultural Industry and 335 National Cultural Industry Role Model Bases.

In 2015, 60 cartoon and animation have been included into the supporting program for cartoon and animation works that illustrated socialist core values, 46 into the national development and protection program for flagship cartoon and animation works. Brilliant creativity in cartoon and animation has been proactively promoted, and cartoon and animation expos were encouraged to be more professional and market-oriented. The Ministry also encouraged the cartoon and animation works to reach out through new media, supported their growth based on Internet Plus strategy, and promoted the progresses of digital content industry. The Ministry facilitated the submission of original Chinese mobile animation and cartoon standard to the ITU for taking a place international standard-setting procedures. By the end of 2015, there were 730 cartoon and animation enterprises jointly approved by the Ministry of Culture, the Ministry of Finance and the State Administration of Taxation of China, among which 43 were identified as key enterprises.

In 2015, the Ministry of Culture steadily intensified its efforts in fostering culture-related technological innovation as well as its application. 53 projects were included in national programs such as plans to enhance national capacity of cultural science and technology, national cultural and technological progress projects, and projects for the establishment, betterment and revision of culture-related industrial standards. A total of 47 innovative projects in cultural and technological areas were deliberated, reviewed and accomplished. Project management was upgraded to identify and foster arts research programs that were compatible with the trend of time, the national cultural development strategies and innovative in nature. 4 programs were selected as prioritized items and 184 were chosen as annual highlights by Art Disciplines Department of the National Social Science Fund. 71 programs were identified as the annual highlights in MOC's cultural and arts studies. 127 national arts studies programs were reviewed and concluded.

VI. Cultural Heritage Protection

In 2015, the State Administration of Cultural Heritage started to renovate 40 state-level Anti-Japanese War memorial sites, and opened all 113 such memorial sites registered as key state heritages to the public. The first traditional village preservation project covering 51 villages were accomplished, and the second project to protect and develop another 100 was initiated. Substantial progresses have been made in Save Forbidden City Project and the renovation of the historical site of the 6th CPC National Congress in Moscow. In July, 2015, after the inscription of Tusi Sites in the UNESCO World Heritage List, China became a country with 48 World Heritages, ranking second in the world.

By the end of the year, there were 8,676 cultural heritage institutions all over China, an increase of 255 from the previous year. Among these, 3,307 were for the preservation of cultural relics, accounting for 38.1%; and 3,852 were museums [13], accounting for 44.4%. By the end of the year, the number of employees by cultural heritage institutions reached 146,000, a decrease of 2100 compared to the end of the previous year. Among them, 8000 were with senior professional titles, accounting for 5.5%; and 18,313 were with medium-grade professional titles, accounting for 12.5%.

Figure 5: Information of national cultural heritage institutions and employed persons in 2006-2015

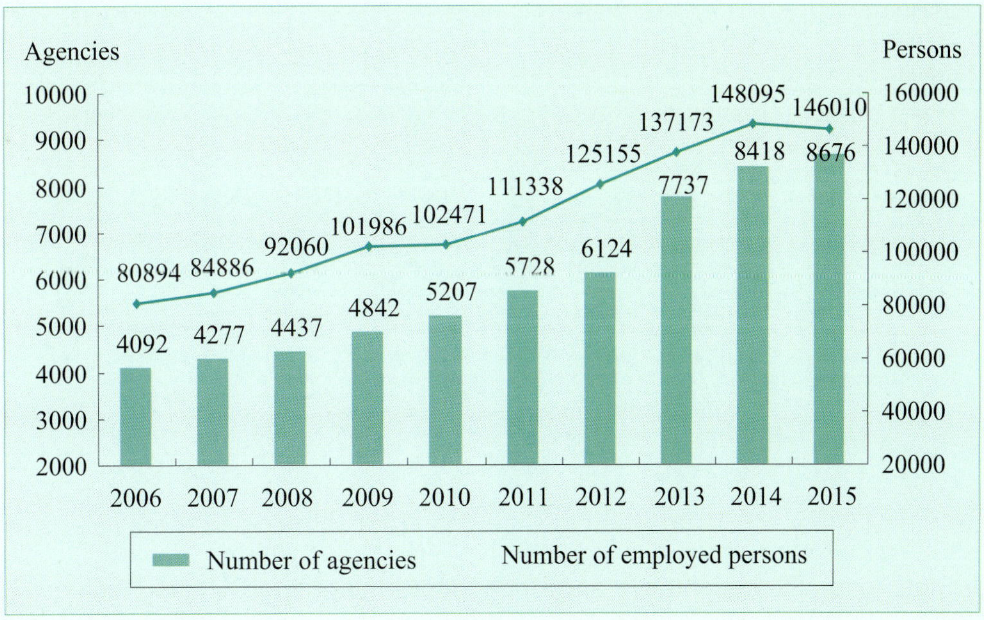

By the end of the year, there were 41.3919 million items of collections of cultural relics in the cultural heritage institutions, an increase of 756,100 since the end of the previous year, or up by 1.9%. Among these, the amount of collections in museums totaled to 30.4414 million, which accounted for 73.5% of the total; and for relics stores, a total of 7.2802 million, accounting for 17.6%. Among these collections, 108,700 were state-level grade-one cultural relics, accounting for

0.3%; 715,400 were state-level grade-two cultural relics, accounting for 1.7%; and 3,888,000 were state-level grade-three cultural relics, accounting for 9.4%. By the end of this year, there were in total 766,700 immovable cultural heritages in China.

Throughout the year, basic exhibitions[14] arranged by cultural heritage institutions reached 10,859 all over China; and temporary exhibitions[15] totaled 11,805; the number of visitor attendances increased to 925.08 million, which was an increase of 9.8% over that of the previous year. Among these, 781.12 million visits were to museums, accounting for 84.4% of the total visits to cultural heritage institutions, up by 8.8%. Among the visitors, the number of minors was 246.63 million, up by 10.1%, accounting for 26.7% of all visitors.

Figure 6: Person-time of audiences and minors to visit heritage institutions cultural in 2008-2015

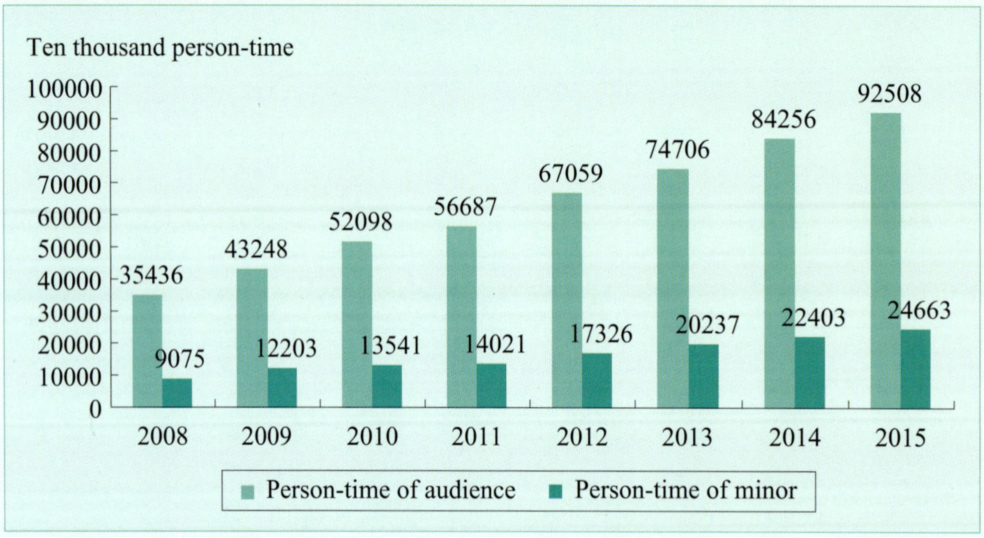

In 2015, the Ministry of Culture enacted the Standard Working Procedures for Inventory of Inheritors of State-level Representative and Endangered Intangible Cultural Heritage (ICH), which provided a framework for including 268 such inheritors into the inventory. 464 state-level ICH were identified and inscribed into the fourth representative list of state-level ICH, and made adjustments and changes to the eligibility of 331 undeserving state-level centers for ICH safeguarding.So far, a total of 1,372 ICH items were announced by the State Council of China as items in the representative list of state-level ICH, and 1,986 inheritors at the same level were identified by the Ministry of Culture. China currently is the country with most entries in the UNESCO lists of ICH, including 30 Chinese items in the UNESCO Representative List of the Intangible Cultural Heritage of Humanity, 7 in the List of Intangible Cultural Heritage in Need of Urgent Safeguarding, and 1 in the Register of Best Safeguarding Practices. According to statistics, by the end of 2015, there were a total of 2,637 safeguarding units[16] for intangible cultural heritage across the country, with 18,657 employees. Throughout the year in the country, these units held 16,937 exhibitions (up by 5.6% compared to that of the previous year)with 32.97 million visitor attendances (down by 2.7%); 39,161 showcases with 39.58 million visitor attendances, up by 12.8% and 4.3% respectively. They hosted 13,567 folklore activities (up by 4.5%) with 37.17 million visitor attendances (down by 4.3%) and 20,588 training classes (down by 1.7%) with 1.51 million attendances of trainees (up by 10.2%) .

VII. Cultural Exchange with Foreign Countries; and Cultural Bonding with Hong Kong, Macao and Taiwan Regions

In 2015, as part of the efforts to implement China's "Belt and Road" initiative, the Ministry of Culture of China hosted major cultural events including the 14th Asia Arts Festival and the 2nd Maritime Silk Road International Arts Festival, the East Asia Cultural Capital nominations, and Cultural Cooperation Forum between China and Central and Eastern European Countries. Major international cultural exchange programs hosted by the Ministry included cultural exchange years between China and Canada and China and the UK, China-US Cultural Forum, China-Russia Cultural Collection, Chinese Cultural Year in South Africa, and Helsinki Arts Festival featuring China as the guest of honor. The Ministry also actively participated in the high-level people-to-people dialogues and intergovernmental dialogues, and made substantial contributions to China's diplomacy.

Local government departments and enterprises were encouraged to engage in the development of overseas China Culture Centers. In 2015, 5 new China Cultural Centers were open overseas, making the total number of such Centers reaching 25. In 2015, these 25 Centers have hosted 221 training classes with 16,036 trainees; 197 lectures with 16,147 visitor attendances; and 924 cultural activities with 2.8014 million visitor attendances.

Aiming to be a flagship cultural event tailored to local demands and markets in different countries, Happy Chinese New Year celebrations have unrolled more than 900 cultural activities in 119 countries and districts all across the globe.

Stronger presence and influence of Beijing, Shanghai and Shenzhen international cultural trade bases were visible. The Ministry further redefined its functions and made some adjustments to the authorization of approving Taiwan cultural dialogue programs to visit the Chinese mainland. The Ministry successfully hosted the hands-on cultural experiences for Hong Kong and Macau college students, cultural field trips for Guangdong, Hong Kong and Macau youths, visiting program for Hong Kong and Macao cultural and art professionals with the special focus on seeking roots along the Silk Road, and dialogues between literary circles from Chinese mainland and Taiwan, which were all platforms for youths from Chinese mainland, Taiwan, Hong Kong and Macau to conduct in-depth cultural and intellectual exchange. The Ministry also hosted 'Root and Soul' ICH presentations, and Chinese New Year and Mid-Autumn Day celebrations, as well as Beijing Culture Temple Fair in Taiwan to promote fraternity and cohesiveness among all compatriots and bring them closer to the roots of Chinese culture.

The year saw 1,667 international cultural exchange programs approved by government cultural departments with 40,781 participant attendances; 230 cultural bonding programs with Hong Kong and Macau, with 5,539 participant attendances, and 500 cultural bonding programs with Taiwan with 12,593 participant attendances.

VIII. Investment in Culture

In 2015, the central budget of China continued to subsidize local culture by implementing cultural projects, such as free access to museums, libraries, and cultural centers (stations). It provided special funding in total 4,780 million yuan, up by 2.7% compared to that of the previous year.

Figure 7: Information of subvention of central budget to local cultural projects in 2006-2015

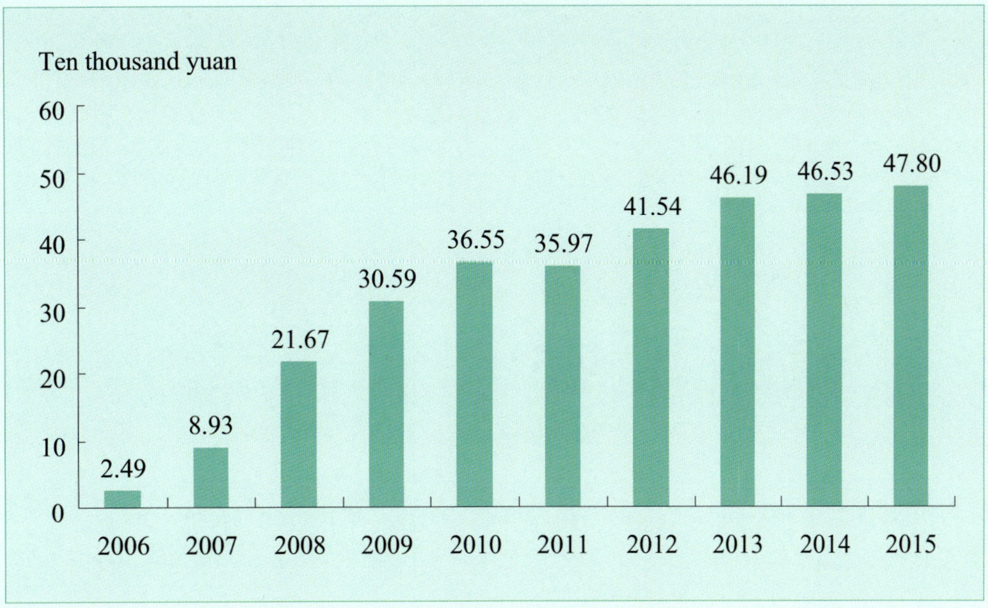

The total amount of cultural undertaking expenses[17] for the whole year was 68.297 billion yuan, an increase of 9.953 billion yuan over that of the previous year, up by 17.1%, 7.1 percentage points higher in growth rate compared to that of the previous year; as for the national cultural undertaking expenses per capita, the total was 49.68 yuan, an increase of 7.03 yuan over the previous year, up by 16.5%.

Figure 8: Information of cultural undertaking expenses per capita in 2006-2015

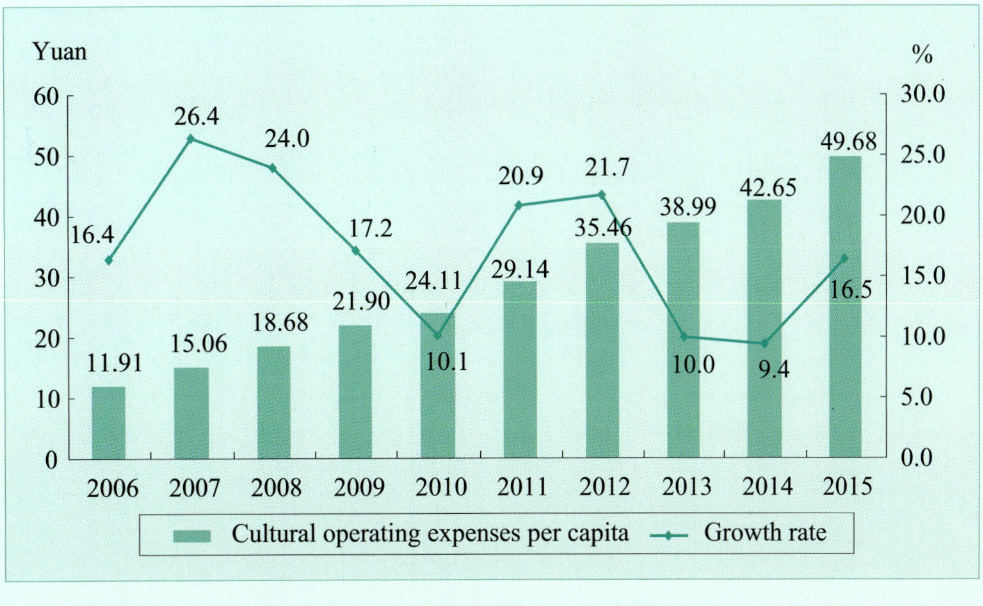

The national cultural undertaking expenses accounted for 0.39% of the country's total financial expenditure, 0.01 percentage points higher than that of the previous year.

Figure 9: Proportion of national cultural undertaking expense in financial expenditure

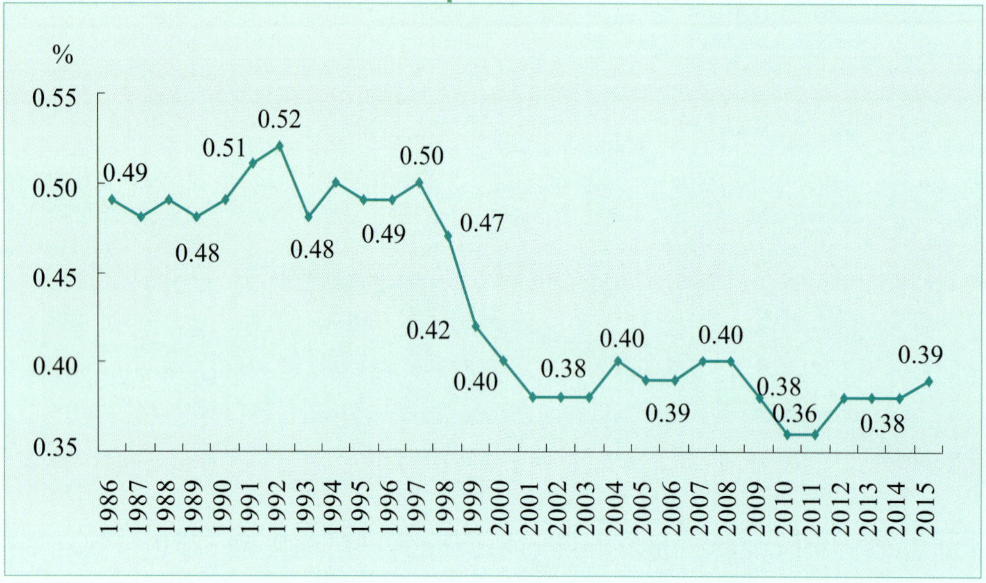

Regarding the national cultural undertaking expenses, that of cultural units above county level was 35.284 billion yuan, accounting for 51.7%, 1.6 percentage points higher than that of the previous year; that of cultural units of county level or below the level of county was 33.013 billion yuan, accounting for 48.3%, down by 1.6 percentage points in the sense of its proportion. The cultural undertaking expenses of eastern region[18] reached 28.787 billion yuan, accounting for 42.1%, and its proportion increased by 0.5%; that of central region reached 16.427 billion yuan, accounting for 24.1%, its proportion increased by 1.2%; and that of western region reached 19.387 billion yuan, accounting for 28.4%, its proportion decreased by 0.9%.

Table 4: Urban & Rural and Regional-based distribution of national cultural undertaking expenses

		In 1995	In 2000	In 2005	In 2010	In 2013	In 2014	In 2015
Aggregate (one hundred million yuan)	**Nationwide**	**33.39**	**63.16**	**133.82**	**323.06**	**530.49**	**583.44**	**682.97**
	# Above county level	24.44	46.33	98.12	206.65	272.67	292.12	352.84
	County level and below level of county	8.95	16.87	35.70	116.41	257.82	291.32	330.13
	# Eastern region	13.43	28.85	64.37	143.35	231.41	242.98	287.87
	Central region	9.54	15.05	30.58	78.65	120.01	133.46	164.27
	Western region	8.30	13.70	27.56	85.78	152.16	171.15	193.87
Proportion (%)	**Nationwide**	**100.0**	**100.0**	**100.0**	**100.0**	**100.0**	**100.0**	**100.0**
	# Above county level	73.2	73.4	73.3	64.0	51.4	50.1	51.7
	County level and below level of county	26.8	26.7	26.7	36.0	48.6	49.9	48.3
	# Eastern region	40.2	45.7	48.1	44.4	43.6	41.6	42.1
	Central region	28.6	23.8	22.9	24.3	22.6	22.9	24.1
	Western region	24.9	21.7	20.6	26.6	28.7	29.3	28.4

The amount of maintenance expenses of national cultural heritage[19] was 28.037 billion yuan, an increase of 3.250 billion yuan, up by 13.1% over that of the previous year; the maintenance expenses of national cultural heritage accounted for 0.16% of China's total financial expenditures, and the proportion was down by 0.01 percentage points over that of the previous year.

According to the Ministry of Finance of China, of the national financial expenditure in 2015, the amount of expenditure for culture, sports and media[20] was 306.7 billion yuan, up by 11.4% over that of the previous year and accounting for 1.74% of the total financial expenditure, and the proportion was down by 0.03 percentage points over that of the previous year.

Figure 10: Aggregate and growth rate of expenditure of national undertakings of culture , sports and media in 2006-2015

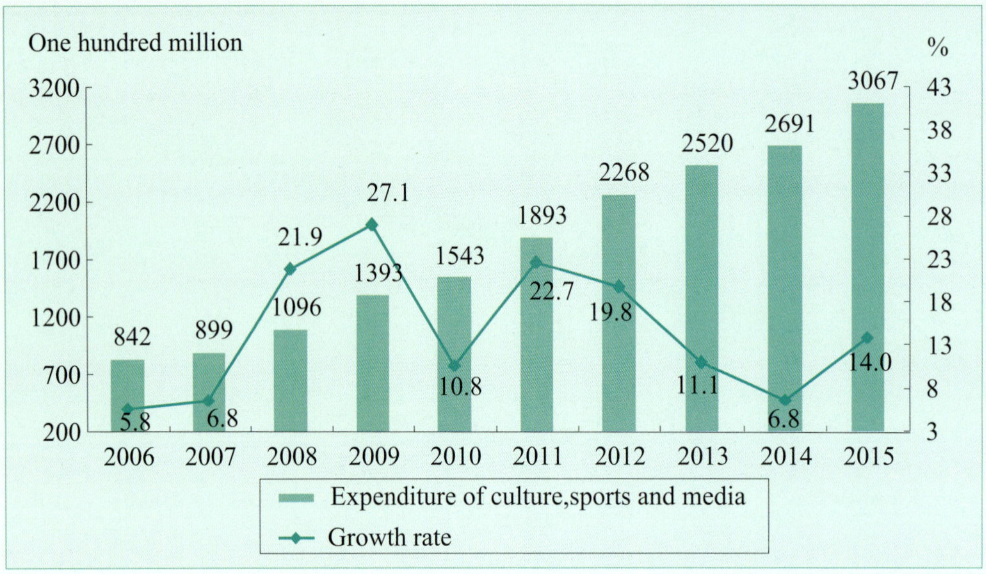

Notes:

[1] All the data of the communiqué are preliminary statistical data. HKSAR, MSAR, and Taiwan Province are not included in each data. Some of data are not compatible with the total of subentries due to rounding off.

[2] Cultural unit refers to cultural institutions that national cultural departments (including cultural system and cultural relic system) of all levels organize or implement industrial management, excluding cultural institutions organized or managed by the departments of all levels of press and publications, radio , film and television, etc. According to the current statistical system, the cultural institutions (such as public libraries, cultural centers, cultural stations, museums, etc.) organized by cultural departments are brought into the statistical range. Regarding cultural institutions with industrial management, the private art performance troupes, cybercafé, and entertainment venues are brought into statistical range, while the mechanism of exchange of works of art, internet culture institution are not in the range.

[3] The employees refer to the people who work and receive working rewards in the institutions that cultural departments at all levels (including cultural systems and cultural relic systems) organize or implement industrial management. The statistical range is ditto with cultural institutions.

[4] The art performance troupes mean various professional artistic performance organizations which are organized by cultural institutions or to which the cultural institutions implement industrial management (with approval of cultural administration department and commercial performance license), and is engaged in such activities as performing arts.

[5] Public library refers to all kinds of institutions that are organized by cultural departments at all levels, and is open to public as well as providing popularization and education of science, culture, and other knowledge.

[6] The total collection of books in public libraries refers to the sum of audiovisual literature materials including bound volume, manual, manuscript, micro-reproduction, videotape, audio tape and CD of ancient books, books, periodicals and newspapers in catalogue. It does not include digital books.

[7] The number of library cards issued refers to the number of library cards which are issued

by public libraries and used at least once in that very year.

[8] The total flow of person-time of public library refers to the gross person-time of receiving the service of the libraries in that year, including borrowing books, consultation and participating in various readers' activities.

[9] The cultural institutions for mass public and communities refer to the places that cultural departments at all levels organize for mass cultural activities, mainly including cultural centers (including comprehensive cultural center and mass art gallery) and cultural stations.

[10] The number of activities means the sum of the organizations of cultural literary and artistic activities, training classes, exhibitions, and public lectures.

[11] The literature and art groups refer to performance teams composed by the staff of this institution and that provide performances for the mass.

[12] The operating units of cultural markets refer to the agencies which are approved or filed by administrative departments of cultural markets and have relevant licenses and filing documents, and that engage in cultural management and services. In line with the current statistical systems, the statistical range of operating units of the cultural market only include private art performance troupes, entertainment venues, and business sites of internet access services.

[13] The museum refers to the non-profit and permanent social service institution which collects, preserves, and exhibits the witness of human activity and natural environment with intent of research, education, and appreciation, as well as being open to the public. It includes the units that carry out activities with proper names such as museums, memorial halls, science and technology museums, exhibition halls, etc.

[14] The permanent exhibition refers to the exhibition which is displayed in the pavilion, with fixed location and for an extended time.

[15] The temporary exhibition means the multi-formed exhibition which is set in the institution and designed by the pavilion.

[16] The intangible cultural heritage safeguarding institutions refer to the protection centers of intangible cultural heritage or protection offices of intangible cultural heritage of all levels.

[17] Cultural undertaking expense means aggregate of expenditures that the finance of

all levels in the area invests to the organizer of cultural systems. It generally includes financial appropriation (excluding appropriations of capital construction costs) of cultural institutions such as art performance troupes, public libraries, cultural centers (stations), etc. and financial subsidies of enterprises subordinate to the Ministry of Culture. According to current statistical caliber, cultural operating expense does not include administrative operation expenditures of cultural administration and management departments at all levels.

[18] Eastern region includes Beijing, Tianjin, Liaoning Province, Shanghai, Jiangsu Province, Fujian Province, Shandong Province, and Guangdong Province; Central region includes Hebei Province, Shanxi Province, Jilin Province, Heilongjiang Province, Anhui Province, Jiangxi Province, Henan Province, Hubei Province, Hunan Province and Hainan Province; Western region includes Inner Mongolia (autonomous region), Guangxi Province, Chongqing, Sichuan Province, Guizhou Province, Yunan Province, Tibet (autonomous region), Shannxi Province, Gansu Province, Qinghai Province, Ningxia (autonomous region), and Xinjiang (autonomous region).

[19] The maintenance expenses of national cultural heritage refer to the aggregate of expenditures that the finance departments at all levels in the area invest to the operation of cultural relics. It generally includes financial appropriation (excluding appropriation of capital construction) of operation institutions of cultural relic such as museum, protection and management agencies for cultural relics, etc. and financial subsidies of enterprises subordinate to cultural relic departments.

[20] The data of expenditure of culture, sports and media, which originates from the Ministry of Finance, is the investment of government at all levels in culture, cultural relics, sports, radio, film and television, and press and publications.